For Sue Lafferty —
"Enjoy!"
— Tom Andrews
HSSC

EL ALISAL
WHERE HISTORY LINGERS

EL ALISAL

WHERE HISTORY LINGERS

BY JANE APOSTOL

Historical Society of Southern California
Los Angeles

Library of Congress Catalog Card Number: 94-076725

ISBN 0-914421-12-3

Designed by Ward Ritchie
Title page illustration from an etching by Orpha Klinker
Cover illustration from a drawing by John Feeley

Printed in the United States of America
by Premier Printing Corporation/Sultana Press, Brea, California

Foreword

Charles Fletcher Lummis walked from Ohio to California, arriving in Los Angeles on February 1, 1885. Fifteen months before his heralded arrival, the Historical Society of Southern California (HSSC) had its beginnings in Los Angeles, founded by another transplanted midwesterner, Noah Levering of Iowa.

Today, more than a century later, the story comes full circle as the Historical Society, which has occupied the Lummis Home as its headquarters since 1965, publishes this thoughtfully written and engagingly illustrated introduction to the man who served as the impresario of the "Arroyo Culture." The Historical Society is especially pleased to have Jane Apostol, author of centennial histories of South Pasadena, HSSC, and Vroman's, apply her talents to one more Arroyo story.

Charles Lummis has resurfaced in recent years as a subject of considerable historical interest. Larger than life at times, full of contradictions at times, certainly unorthodox with a flair for the dramatic, Lummis has long been shrouded in myth and half-truths. He can now step forward as Jane Apostol concisely and accurately introduces both the man and his beloved El Alisal.

Once Lummis had safely arrived here, he was fond of saying that "God made California and He made it on purpose." I suspect, however, that those

7

who came to know this energetic and theatrical author, editor, librarian, curator, scholar, preservationist, and booster might have found it difficult to apply the same reasoning to Lummis himself.

But no matter. As Jane Apostol ably points out, Lummis accomplished a great deal in his nearly three score and ten years. His perceptive and skillful recording of the southwestern scene, for example, earned him praise from Lawrence Clark Powell as the "one against whom all subsequent Southwesterners must be measured."

In *El Alisal: Where History Lingers*, you are invited to share in his adventures and crusades, to partake of the hospitality of his house, to mingle with his guests and neighbors—and to do some measuring of your own.

The Historical Society of Southern California is pleased to acknowledge The Ahmanson Foundation for believing in this project and supporting it with a generous grant and Premier Printing Corporation for donating generously to the printing of this book.

To Ward Ritchie, designer; Tom Apostol, photographer and editor; Dana Cordrey, printer; and Jane Apostol, prizewinning local historian, the Historical Society also expresses its sincere thanks and appreciation.

June 1994
El Alisal

THOMAS F. ANDREWS
Executive Director
The Historical Society of Southern California

Table of Contents

List of Illustrations

EL ALISAL
WHERE HISTORY LINGERS

Charles Fletcher Lummis

A plaque on the patio wall of El Alisal, the arroyo boulder house of Charles Fletcher Lummis, lists the accomplishments by which he wanted to be remembered:

> He founded the Southwest Museum
> He built this house
> He saved four old missions
> He studied and recorded Spanish America
> He tried to do his share.

He did his share in an extraordinary number of fields. Lummis was the first city editor of the *Los Angeles Times*, the crusading editor of *Land of Sunshine* and *Out West*, an innovative city librarian, and a prolific author. In addition he was folklorist, photographer, ethnographer, and archaeologist. As

Charles Fletcher Lummis as a Harvard freshman.
Courtesy of Huntington Library.

16

his friend Edgar L. Hewett, director of the School of American Research, wrote in *Lummis the Inimitable,* he was "many lived, myriad minded, golden hearted."

Charles Fletcher Lummis was born March 1, 1859, in Lynn, Massachusetts. Taught by his father (a Methodist minister and classics scholar), the boy could read Latin, Greek, and Hebrew by the age of ten. At eighteen he entered Harvard and helped pay his way through college by his first best-seller, a miniature booklet called *Birch Bark Poems.* Lummis wrote the poems, printed them on birch bark with a handpress, and eventually sold more than fourteen thousand copies. (One purchaser was Theodore Roosevelt, a fellow student at Harvard.)

Although Lummis did not finish his senior year at Harvard (where he majored, he said, in Poker, Poetry, and Athletics), the college awarded him his degree when the Class of 1881 celebrated its twenty-fifth anniversary. During his junior year Lummis married a young medical student, Dorothea Rhodes. While she remained in Boston to complete her studies, he left for Ohio to try managing his father-in-law's farm in the Scioto Valley. It was a short-lived experiment that Lummis abandoned for a job as city editor, and then as editor-in-chief, of the oldest paper west of the Alleghenies, the *Scioto Gazette* in Chillicothe. He enjoyed running the paper, but eager for new sights and experiences (or, as one biographer put it, to escape malaria and monotony), he decided to go to California — and to walk the whole way. The *Los Angeles Daily Times* arranged to publish his cross-country reports

Lummis in 1885, at the conclusion of his trek from
Ohio to California. Copies of the picture ("Lummis
in full traveling costume") were available from
the *Chillicothe Leader* for fifty cents.
Courtesy of Keith Lummis.

18

(at five dollars for each weekly letter) and to hire him upon his arrival in town.

On September 12, 1884, Lummis set out on the 3,507-mile trek he would describe as "a happy vagabondizing" in *A Tramp Across the Continent,* his exuberant account of the journey. After traveling through seven states and two territories in 143 days, he reached Los Angeles on February 1, 1885, accompanied for the last eleven miles by *Times* publisher Harrison Gray Otis, who met him at Mission San Gabriel. Newspaper accounts had made Lummis something of a folk hero; and the *Chillicothe Leader* advertised souvenir photos that showed him with a serape over one shoulder and a six-shooter tucked in his belt. The *Times* for February 3, 1885, devoted more than a column to the arrival of the "plucky pedestrian," and a later issue of the paper announced that Lummis had joined the staff. Although the city desk was his main responsibility, in 1886 he spent three months in Arizona Territory, covering General George Crook's campaign against the Chiricahua Apache leader, Geronimo. Lummis admired qualities in both men, and later critics have praised his dispatches for their perceptiveness and objectivity.

Endowed with formidable energy and drive, Lummis prided himself on being able to work almost around the clock, with only a few hours of sleep each night. Then in December 1887, not yet twenty-nine years old, he suffered a paralytic stroke that affected his left arm and side. Determined to cure himself he returned to New Mexico, whose land and people had captivated him on his westward

An Isleta girl, Reyes Chirina, photographed by Lummis
in 1888. He included a transparency of the picture in his
photographic window at El Alisal. *Courtesy of
Southwest Museum, Los Angeles. N24488.*

trek in 1884. He stayed first at the hacienda of his friend Amado Chaves, Speaker of the Territorial Legislature of New Mexico; then moved to a small adobe in the Rio Grande pueblo of Isleta. Following a self-prescribed regimen, Lummis forced himself to walk, to ride horseback, and with his one good arm to handle a gun, a camera, and a fishing rod — and to roll his own cigarettes. He was, he boasted, a rather lively paralytic. Some of his lively activity was intellectual. He studied Spanish and also the Tiwa language of his Isleta neighbors, memorized ballads sung for him by Mexican shepherds, and wrote down the Pueblo legends that he heard. He photographed his Pueblo friends, daringly photographed secret Penitente rituals (the first person to do so), and in the company of archaeologist and historian Adolph Bandelier took the first pictures of the ruins at what is now Bandelier National Monument (and where a peak has been named for Lummis). Toward the end of his stay in Isleta, Lummis fought a successful battle for Indian rights. A son of Juan Rey Abeita, his friend and landlord, was forcibly removed from the pueblo in 1892 to be educated in the government's Indian school at Albuquerque. Lummis filed a writ of *habeas corpus* and secured the boy's return, along with that of more than thirty other Isleta children.

Between 1891 and 1898 Lummis published ten books, most of them inspired by New Mexico. Perhaps best known is his classic, *The Land of Poco Tiempo*. Its dedication, "To Eva and Dorothea," pays tribute to his first wife, Dorothea Rhodes; and his second wife, Eva Frances Douglas. (Both mar-

Charles and Eve Lummis, their daughter Turbesé, and Luis Abieta, son of an Isleta friend. *Courtesy of Southwest Museum, Los Angeles. N10276.*

riages ended in divorce.) Dorothea was one of the first women doctors in Los Angeles, president of the Los Angeles County Homeopathic Medical Society, and founder of the Society for Prevention of Cruelty to Children. Eva (or Eve, as her friends called her) was a teacher in the Isleta mission school when she and Lummis met. Eve later won recognition as a translator of Spanish literature and was awarded an honorary doctorate of letters by the University of Arizona.

Lummis married young Eve Douglas in March 1891, and their daughter Turbesé was born in Isleta the following June. Four months later Lummis settled his wife and child in Los Angeles, packed his bulky view camera, and joined Bandelier on an archaeological expedition to South America. "I had the honor to be the handy-man," Lummis said with unaccustomed modesty. In Peru he helped with excavations at the pre-Incan site of Pachacamac and photographed the finds. In Bolivia he made the best early photographs of the great monolithic gateway and enormous stone sculptures at Tiahuanaco. Calling it the chance of a lifetime, he also explored much of the countryside, from the depths of a canyon to the top of a nineteen-thousand-foot volcano.

Funding for the expedition came to an end in 1893, and Lummis returned to Los Angeles at the end of the year. Soon he accepted a new challenge: to become editor (with absolute control) of the fledgling *Land of Sunshine,* a slim monthly publication addressed to "travelers, health seekers, and intending settlers." Sole editor from January 1895

23

Cover designed by Gutzon Borglum, who is best known
for his sculptures on Mount Rushmore. *Courtesy
of Southwest Museum, Los Angeles. N41958.*

until February 1903 and coeditor until his resignation in November 1909, Lummis transformed a
booster journal into a noteworthy publication that
included President Theodore Roosevelt and natu-
ralist John Muir among its subscribers. "I have read
your little plucky magazine & like it," Muir wrote to
Lummis in 1895. "It has the ring & look of true literary metal."

Lummis once jokingly remarked that in *Land of
Sunshine* people could read about "orange crops,
frontier stories, Indian policies, Western history,
[and] climate as a means of grace." They also could
discover the work of new writers like Mary Austin
and new artists like Maynard Dixon and Ed Borein,
learn about the latest books and what Lummis
thought of them, and read his provocative editorial
section, "In the Lion's Den." There he battled for
causes ranging from the conservation of natural
resources to the correct pronunciation of Los
Angeles. ("The Lady would remind you, *please*, Her
name is *not* LOST ANGIE LEES.") With equal fervor he
attacked imperialism, simplified ("deformed")
spelling, and the government's treatment of Native
Americans.

Land of Sunshine (renamed *Out West* in 1902) gave
valuable publicity to two crusading organizations
founded by Lummis: the Landmarks Club and the
Sequoya League. The Landmarks Club, a pioneer
among preservation groups, incorporated in 1895 to
help rescue from decay California's old Franciscan
missions ("the noblest ruins in the United States").
With money from dues, contributions, and fund-
raising projects, the club paid for essential repairs to

At Mission San Juan Capistrano, which the Landmarks Club helped preserve. The noted photographer of the West, William Henry Jackson, took this picture of Lummis, Turbesé, and the sacristan in 1899. *Courtesy of Southwest Museum, Los Angeles. N24349.*

the missions at San Juan Capistrano, San Diego, and San Fernando, and to the *asistencia* at Pala, an outlying branch of Mission San Luis Rey. Some of the money raised came from sale of the *Landmarks Club Cook Book*, to which Lummis contributed forty-two recipes, an essay on Spanish-American cookery, and photographs documenting the state of the missions before and after repairs.

Out West also publicized the work of the Sequoya League, founded by Lummis in 1901 to help change the government's Indian policy (which he described as "Remote, Uninformed, Unhuman, and Unsatisfactory"). In its first campaign the Sequoya League sought justice for some three hundred Cupeño Indians who were to be evicted from their ancestral home on Warner's Ranch in San Diego County. As a result of untiring efforts by the League and an advisory commission chaired by Lummis, the Indians were resettled in the nearby Pala valley on a large tract of fertile land. Destitute Campo Indians also benefited from efforts of the Sequoya League, which organized emergency relief, provided a market for Campo baskets, and lobbied successfully to provide the Campos with productive acreage. Subsequent reforms in the government's Indian policy owe much to the Sequoya League, its support of Indian rights, and its respect for Indian culture and religion.

In 1903 Lummis founded yet another organization. This was the Southwest Society, a branch of the Archaeological Institute of America. One of its goals was to build a museum in Los Angeles. "Not an old Curiosity Shop of jumbles from God-knows-

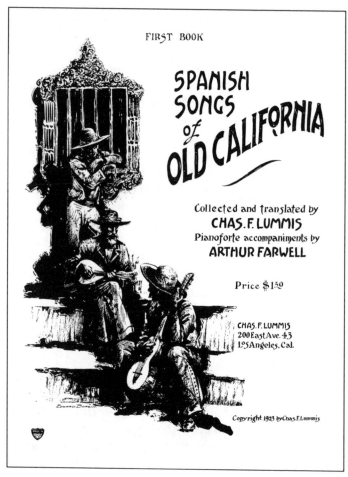

FIRST BOOK

SPANISH
SONGS
of
OLD CALIFORNIA

Collected and translated by
CHAS. F. LUMMIS
Pianoforte accompaniments by
ARTHUR FARWELL

Price $1.50

CHAS. F. LUMMIS
200 East Ave. 43
Los Angeles, Cal.

Copyright 1923 by Chas. F. Lummis

A cover by cowboy artist Ed Borein, whose first drawings for *Land of Sunshine* appeared in 1899. Borein and his wife were married at El Alisal in 1921. *HSSC Collection.*

where," said Lummis, "but a Museum which can compare with any in the world in everything but bulk." Within a year the Southwest Society had built an impressive membership and acquired valuable collections of early California books, paintings, and Indian artifacts. It also had launched the imaginative project Lummis described as "catching our Archaeology alive." This was the recording of *Californio* and Native American songs to preserve music that might otherwise be forgotten. By 1905, using an Edison Home Phonograph, the society had made wax-cylinder recordings of more than four hundred and fifty songs. Most were in Spanish, but a hundred were in twenty-five American Indian languages. *Spanish Songs of Old California*, published in 1923 and since reprinted, contains the words and music of fourteen songs collected and translated by Lummis. "I feel that we who today inherit California are under a filial obligation to save whatever we may of the incomparable Romance which has made the word California a word to conjure with for 400 years," Lummis wrote in his preface. "I feel that we cannot decently dodge a certain trusteeship to save the Old Missions from ruin and the Old Songs from oblivion."

In 1905, although still an editor of *Out West* and a mainstay of the Southwest Society, Lummis embarked on a new career. "Attired in his corduroys, peek-a-boo shirt and cowboy hat, and grasping his striped canvas grab-bag," the *Los Angeles Times* reported on June 28, "Charles F. Lummis took the oath of office as City Librarian." The event was newsworthy, not only because of

The Los Angeles Public Library roof garden — a Lummis innovation. *Courtesy of Southwest Museum, Los Angeles.* P14701.

Lummis's trademark costume, but because of the circumstances of his appointment. Deciding that a man should head the library, the board fired the incumbent, Mary Jones, and named Lummis to succeed her. "We did not know," said one indignant woman, "that the best qualification for a librarian was accurate knowledge of the aborigines." Librarians across the country protested the board's action, but Lummis proved a capable and creative administrator. His first reforms ranged from installing water coolers to raising salaries; from branding the top edge of library books to hiring a "living encyclopedia" as head of a new Department of Reading, Study, and Research. By 1910, when Lummis resigned, he had established a Library Senate, founded a Department of Western History Material, built up the reference and rare book collections, and presided over two moves of the library into larger quarters (each time arranging for a rooftop reading room). He also happily launched The Bibliosmiles: A Rally of Librarians Who Are Nevertheless Human.

As city librarian, Lummis produced lively and informative annual reports that were required reading in some library schools. "Mr. Lummis writes with magnetism, strong convictions and with a breeziness not usually characteristic of official documents," commented the *Library Journal* in 1907. Of his final report as city librarian the *Journal* observed, "Although Mr. Lummis's report cannot be said to be fettered by the chains of conventional modesty . . . the record of the actual work done so far as it is indicated here and there, seems to be con-

What we are here for

BY CHARLES F. LUMMIS, CITY LIBRARIAN OF LOS ANGELES

*My instructions to this staff, many times repeated,
with reference to the general character
of the institution have been:*

"WE HAVE FOUND NO MILLIONAIRES; we cannot expect to compete in books and binding with the richest libraries in the greatest cities, with their $5,000,000 buildings and $5,000,000 stock. All that depends upon liberalities beyond our control. But we can have, and I wish you to help me to make, the best library in the world, not only of its size but of any size, in the cheerfulness, courtesy, accuracy, and promptness with which every patron is given what he desires of anything this library has. Don't wait for anyone to wake you up—*look* for a chance to be helpful. We do not have to ask any rich man to give us that. It is in our own hands. If anyone becomes impatient with you, that is the time for you to be patient. If you meet discourtesy, increase your own manners. The best capital in the world, in any profession, is consideration. It is also the first duty of all who serve the public. Don't hurry, don't worry; and never stop growing."

This excerpt from the *Librarian's Annual Report* for 1906, designed and printed by Lawton Kennedy of San Francisco, March 1956, as SOUTHWEST BROADSIDE NUMBER 7, for the friends of Lawrence Clark Powell.

HSSC Collection.

siderable." A history of Los Angeles city librarians by author and bibliographer John Bruckman describes Lummis as "innovative, intuitive, erudite, sometimes erratic and always impatient. . . . When all is said and done, however, in spite of the alarums and confusions attendant on his stewardship, Lummis added an indefinable something to the library which can only be characterized as 'quality.' He found it good, and left it great."

Lummis's resignation in March 1910 was unexpected. It came about, according to the *Los Angeles Times*, because of philosophic differences with the mayor and with members of the library board who wanted more attention paid to the general reader and less to the research scholar. Lummis said only that he was resigning to devote more time to writing and "to the preservation of our missions, the needs of our Indians, and the upbuilding of a great museum." Fifty-one years old at the time of his resignation, Lummis celebrated his birthday with a splendid gesture. For the sum of one dollar he deeded to the Southwest Museum (which was as yet unbuilt) his valuable library of five thousand books and manuscripts; the exhaustive card catalog of his projected Dictionary-Concordance-Encyclopedia of Spanish America; and his remarkable collections of photographs, paintings, Navajo blankets, and prehistoric artifacts. In addition he arranged to leave to the museum his distinctive, handcrafted house, El Alisal, which was less than a mile away, close to the Arroyo Seco. Expressing gratitude for his largesse, the museum bestowed on Lummis the rather curious title of Founder Emeritus.

The Southwest Museum around 1920, when the elevator was
under construction. In the foreground is one of the yellow
trolley cars of the Los Angeles Railway. *Courtesy of
Southwest Museum, Los Angeles. N32167.*

In 1911 Lummis suffered temporary blindness, possibly from jungle fever contracted earlier that year during excavations of Mayan ruins in Guatemala. His eyes were still bandaged when he took part in groundbreaking ceremonies for the Southwest Museum on November 16, 1912. Lummis not only chose the hilltop site, which commanded a view from the San Gabriel Mountains to the sea, but he worked with architect Sumner Hunt on every detail of the museum, from the location of exhibit cases to the design of the great caracol tower, with its spiral staircase of 160 steps. Even temporary blindness did not keep Lummis from the drafting table. He had his fingers guided over the plans, then indicated to Hunt the changes and corrections he felt were necessary.

Lummis took joy in the museum at a time when his personal world was far from happy. His second wife, Eve, left him in 1909, taking two of their children with her: sixteen-year-old Turbesé and four-year-old Keith. Only nine-year-old Jordan (known also by his Indian name, Quimu) stayed with his father. (A fourth child, Amado Bandelier, had died in 1900.) In 1915 Lummis married again (his third wife was Gertrude Redit, who had been his secretary), but this marriage, too, ended in divorce.

The Southwest Museum opened its doors to the public on August 1, 1914. "It is a marvel," Lummis wrote, "how truly it realizes my dream." Although rich in holdings, the museum had little more than fifty dollars in the bank. Board members disagreed over fund-raising methods; and there was friction, also, over Lummis's desire to establish satellite

35

Lummis with friends at the Enchanted Mesa, near Acoma,
New Mexico, in June 1898. The photograph was taken by
Jessie Knight Jordan, wife of the first president
of Stanford University. *Courtesy of Southwest
Museum, Los Angeles.* N24352B.

museums throughout the Southwest. "I resigned as Secretary of the Southwest Museum March 11, 1915," he wrote indignantly, "on the plea of dear friends on the board who thought Money Interests were more important." He finished out his term as a trustee, but was not reelected to the institution he had founded. In 1923, however, the Southwest Museum recognized Lummis's sixty-fourth birthday with a gala Founder's Day celebration at which the most dramatic feature of the building was dedicated as the Lummis Caracol Tower. Another honor that he cherished came in 1915 when King Alfonso XIII of Spain named Lummis a Knight Commander, with the impressive title *Comendador con placa de la Real Orden de Isabel la Católica.*

During the summers of 1926 and 1927 Lummis made two final visits to his beloved New Mexico, whose landscape he once summed up with the words "Sun, Silence, and Adobe." He climbed again to the mesa-top pueblo of Acoma, which he had photographed more than a quarter of a century earlier; he took part in activities of the School of American Research at Santa Fe, of which he was a founding board member; and he spoke before a gathering of Pueblo leaders who had asked his advice on their problems with the government. Lummis "had taken their hearts," said one Native American, who was quoted as saying also that no finer talk had ever been made before an Indian council.

In November 1927 Lummis learned that he had cancer and no more than a year to live. With characteristic resolve he attacked three projects he was

37

Lummis at El Alisal. The photograph behind him, taken in
1903, shows Lummis with President Theodore Roosevelt,
his friend since Harvard days. *HSSC Collection.*

determined to finish. One was revising *The Spanish Pioneers*, which he first published in 1893. Another was seeing through the press a collection of his essays, gathered together as *Flowers of Our Lost Romance*. Both volumes came out posthumously. Lummis also wanted to publish a collection of his verse. "This book of poems, if not most important, will sort of ease my mind," he noted in his journal. Houghton Mifflin accepted the manuscript of *A Bronco Pegasus* and sent him an advance copy of the published book just two weeks before his death.

Lummis died on November 25, 1928. Several hundred friends gathered at El Alisal a few days later for a brief service beneath a great sycamore in the patio. The valedictory was not a hymn but one of Lummis's favorite songs, *"Adiós, Adiós, Amores."* Novelist Eugene Manlove Rhodes, who owed his first appearance in print to Lummis, wrote in final tribute to his friend: "In twenty ways Lummis was the most remarkable man I ever knew — his scholarly thoroughness, his appalling industry, his rapier-like wit, and the militant heart that never feared to make a foe in a good cause. He finished what he started, and he paid for what he broke."

El Alisal

The ashes of Charles Fletcher Lummis rest in a niche at El Alisal, the house he built to last one thousand years. Its architecture, he had written, "is part of my life and my brains and my love and my hands." Located a few miles from downtown Los Angeles, at 200 East Avenue 43, the house stands on the west bank of the Arroyo Seco, the usually dry riverbed that arises in the San Gabriel Mountains and extends to the Los Angeles River. Lummis's one-time neighbor, Mary Austin, described the Arroyo as it appeared at the turn of the century. "At most seasons of the year," she wrote, "[it is] a small trickle of water among stones in a wide, deep wash, overgrown with button willow and sycamores. . . . Tiny gold and silver backed ferns climb down the banks to drink, and as soon as the spring freshet has gone by, brodiaeas and blazing stars come up between the boulders worn as smooth as if by hand."

Progress shots taken by Lummis at El Alisal in September
1898 and March 1904. *Courtesy of Huntington Library.*

In September 1895 Lummis inspected Arroyo acreage in what then was called Garvanza and now is Highland Park. Drawing the last hundred dollars from his bank account, he made a down payment on three acres of land in the Sycamore Grove Tract, a subdivision of the old Verdugo Rancho. As Lummis described his parcel, "It was covered with brush, gravel, granite boulders and thirty noble sycamores." A magnificent tree with a fourfold trunk inspired the name El Alisal: the local Spanish for Place of the Sycamore.

Exactly three years after buying the land, Lummis noted in his diary, "Begin Big House." Building around the great tree, he painstakingly erected the L-shaped house that he called his stone castle. Made of concrete and faced with arroyo boulders, it boasts a circular tower thirty feet tall, a scroll-topped bell cote (or *espadaña*), and lattice-work chimneys like one at Mission San Juan Capistrano. Lummis did most of the work on El Alisal himself: hauling boulders, laying foundations, putting up walls, and fashioning cupboards, shelves, and doors. "The creative thrill is so fine and keen," he said, "it is sheer pitiful to see a man get a home off the bargain counter, and miss nearly all the joy he might just as well have of it."

Lummis was not without experience as a carpenter. While convalescing in New Mexico (as he wrote in *My Friend Will*, the third-person account of his battle against paralysis), "He even built a couple of log houses for friends who had taken the crazy notion to plant a home on the top of a ten-thousand-foot peak; felling the trees himself, peel-

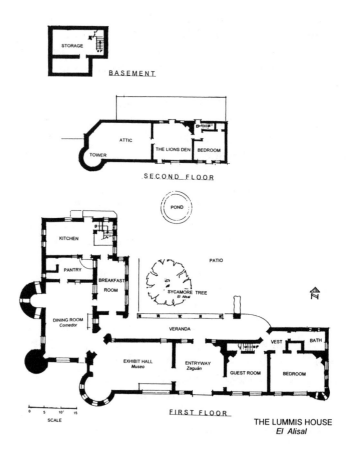

BASEMENT

STORAGE

ATTIC

TOWER

THE LIONS DEN BEDROOM

SECOND FLOOR

POND

KITCHEN

PANTRY

PATIO

BREAKFAST
ROOM

SYCAMORE TREE
El Alisal

DINING ROOM
Comedor

VERANDA

VEST BATH

EXHIBIT HALL
Museo

ENTRYWAY
Zaguán

GUEST ROOM

BEDROOM

0 5 10' 15
SCALE

FIRST FLOOR

THE LUMMIS HOUSE
El Alisal

Drawing by F. Kirk Helm.

44

ing, hewing, and placing them, making tin roofs, and all that sort of thing." He also built a *casita* — a four-room redwood shack — on his arroyo property as a temporary residence until he and his family could move into their new home.

Lummis often worked from daybreak till dark on the construction of El Alisal. In the process he learned new skills. "Damn plastering flies everywhere but to the wall, at first," he admitted on one occasion, "but presently I get it tame and to stick to the wall — and feel right proud." Each year one or two young boys brought from Isleta Pueblo helped with some of the tasks; and for specialized jobs like masonry, Lummis turned to professionals. He also worked closely with Sumner Hunt, an architectural advisor to the Landmarks Club and later chief architect of the Southwest Museum. Hunt wrote to Lummis in 1921:

I believe a visit to your house means more to me than it could to most people, because of the reminder of our mutual efforts to create it. Commencing with scraps in the office as to plan and design, which you being [a] forceful chap were allways settled your way, with the resulting charm of the house, then the calls for help from you when problems of construction and finish developed, my frequent trips to the house to show you how, and then your doing it your way, with curiously the still resulting interest and charm. . . . I love the house and your wonderful stuff in it and joy in your joy of the possession of it. Long may it stand, and you with it.

45

The El Alisal *museo:* the large room in which Lummis displayed his collections. *Courtesy of Keith Lummis.*

Lummis did rejoice in his house and its special quality. As he wrote in 1912 to the Los Angeles Park Commission:

The woodwork is massive and all by hand — no mill work. The ceiling beams are 10 x 12 and 8 x 10, all hewn by me with the broad-ax; except two rooms where there are 12-inch cedar logs burned and rubbed. The ceilings are 5-inch redwood, hewn by me with the adze. The casings are massive, no two doors or windows alike; all hewn. Front door weighs a ton. Thinnest door three inches thick. Mostly dovetailed. Floors cement, ceilings fireproofed. Choice woods. Many historic timbers and other articles built in.

The first room that Lummis built — and the largest — is the *museo*, a combination of living room and exhibition hall, twenty-five feet long (twenty-eight feet according to Lummis, who measured into the alcove). Here he displayed his Indian blankets, baskets, pots, and other artifacts, as well as his many paintings by Western artists. In January 1899 Lummis wrote to archaeologist and ethnologist Frederick Webb Hodge: "I've just finished ceiling the big room (28 x 16) in wh[ich] my precious collections & library will be absolutely safe. And won't I draw a long breath when I get them there! All these years they've been in a frame house." Most of the collections now are in the Southwest Museum, but a number of personal items are exhibited in the *museo*. Among them are photographs of friends and family, the machine used by Lummis to make wax-cylinder recordings, and his typewriter with moveable type.

47

The *museo* fireplace, photographed by Lummis in May 1899, shortly after its completion. Lummis kept his pipes and flint in the box on the lower shelf. *Courtesy of Southwest Museum, Los Angeles. P35559.*

48

Like the rest of the house, the *museo* has plastered walls and concrete floors. "Housecleaning has no terrors here," said Lummis, who advised hosing down the interior when it was dirty. Other features of the *museo* are a corner fireplace and an open-beamed ceiling. Described by Lummis as "12-inch cedar logs burned and rubbed," the beams in the *museo* and the adjoining entrance hall were utility poles obtained from the Santa Fe Railroad. The *museo* displays other ingenious uses for the timbers. Two segments, sheathed in copper, frame the fireplace on either side. A third piece forms the mantel, while yet another serves as the pedestal for an Indian basket. Lummis even turned one short length into a container for his pipes and flint.

Perhaps the most distinctive feature of the *museo* is its photographic window. In the apt description of Ron R. Kinsey, former curator of photographs at the Southwest Museum, it is Lummis's "autobiography in glass, a *vita in vitro* of over a decade of his explorations and travels." The window consists of three large panes, each bordered with black and white glass transparencies made from photographs taken by Lummis between 1888 and 1896. Around the windowpane at the left are scenes of Mexico, around the center pane are views of the Southwest, and around the pane at the right are scenes of Bolivia and Peru. Below the photographic window is one of the practical pieces of furniture designed by Lummis: a window seat that opens up for storage.

At one end of the *museo* is a little alcove formed by a wall of the circular tower. Above a curved

The *zaguán*, or entryway, photographed in May 1899, a few months after Lummis moved his desk into the room. *Courtesy of Southwest Museum, Los Angeles. N24261.*

bench in the alcove are three tall windows. The most westerly, placed to catch the last rays of the setting sun, has a wooden inset with the cutout pattern of a sunburst. A detail in "The Maids of Honor," a Velázquez painting admired by Eve, suggested the design in the carved double doors leading from the western end of the *museo* to the dining room.

Even before finishing the *museo*, Lummis began work on the *zaguán*, the entrance hall adjoining it on the east. For the windows of both rooms he made buckskin curtains, fringed with two hundred jingles he had cut from copper and German silver. The task proved difficult. *Con gran trabajo* ("with much work") is a frequent complaint in his diaries, which he kept in a mixture of English and Spanish, with confidential entries spelled out in Greek letters.

Lummis wanted the walls of the *zaguán* to have an ornamental border, inspired by geometric designs on the "mosaic palaces" of Mitla. He abandoned the idea, however, with the rueful confession, "My Mitla stencil defying all efforts to make it work." Lummis was far more successful with his carpentry. "First good door I ever built and really best yet," he said of the door between *zaguán* and patio. He was proud of the careful dovetailing. "Any fool can write a book," he often remarked, "but it takes a man to make a dovetail door."

A gift from Bishop George Montgomery — a plank from Mission San Fernando — adds interest to another door in the *zaguán*. Writing about the gift, Lummis reported: "Clean up original timber

51

Lummis as portrayed by Alexander Harmer on a page of
the House Book signed by guests at El Alisal. *Courtesy
of Southwest Museum, Los Angeles. N24261.*

of San Fernando Mission and I saw one end to square — and ruin a good saw. Panel just as it was hewn by the padres in 1797; but was for 50 years over the smoke-room where they smoked their hams; and it is indurated almost like a fossil. Put it in as panel to E door of Zaguan."

For a brief time the *zaguán* served as Lummis's office, with a William Keith painting on the wall and a rolltop desk the chief item of furniture. The *zaguán* was the setting for the first Christmas tree at El Alisal. (Instead of the usual evergreen, Lummis decorated a pepper tree.) The room was the setting also for the first wedding held at El Alisal: that of Maynard and Lillian Dixon in 1905. A table in the *zaguán* held the great red morocco house book signed by the Dixons and hundreds of other visitors to El Alisal. Artists, actors, writers, musicians, ethnologists, and historians were among those who autographed or illustrated some of the four hundred pages in the book. A few of the familiar names to be found here are those of John Muir, Will Rogers, Helena Modjeska, John Philip Sousa, Frederic Remington, and Carl Sandburg. Cowboy artist Ed Borein drew several sketches in the house book, including one made on his wedding day, when he and Lucile Maxwell were married at El Alisal.

The great front entrance into the *zaguán* is nearly seven feet high with massive double doors, each half weighing about a thousand pounds. The planks are made of yellow pine and red birch ("our native mahogany") and fastened with wrought-iron nails. Fruhling Brothers of Los Angeles, who advertised "artistic wrought iron works," followed

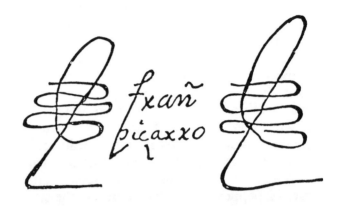

Decorative ironwork on the great front doors of El Alisal, and the *rúbrica* of Pizarro, which inspired the calligraphic design. *Photos by Tom M. Apostol. HSSC Collection.*

designs supplied by Lummis in forging the impressive hardware for the doors. The flowing calligraphic device is a copy of the distinctive flourish — or *rúbrica* — that Francisco Pizarro used with his signature. (Perhaps Lummis saw in the *rúbrica* the first and last initials of his own monogram.) The hinges resemble the condor-headed sceptres carried by a pre-Incan deity. Lummis had photographed a stone carving of the god on a monumental gateway at Tiahuanaco, in the Andes. El Alisal's splendid double doors, completed in the spring of 1899, were used for little more than a year. Then they were locked and bolted, a symbol of the grief that closed in on Lummis when his six-year-old son Amado died on Christmas Day of 1900.

"Am working like a termite on the house," Lummis had written the previous December after finishing a little guest room east of the *zaguán*. Until her own room was built, Eve was ensconced in the guest room, completed by Lummis just three weeks before the birth of Jordan, their second son. The little room is notable for its fireplace, on which Charles Walter Stetson modeled a Navajo fire dance. Lummis composed the couplet inscribed around the fireplace opening:

A casual savage cracked two stones together:
A spark — and Man was armed against the weather.

Carved on a shelf above the fireplace mantel is the old-fashioned greeting, *Buenos días le de Dios* ("May God grant you good days"). A frieze of small clay heads from Teotihuacán, Mexico's ancient City of the Gods, ornaments the mantel. A wooden figurine

55

The guest room at El Alisal, with a bed
built by Lummis. *HSSC Collection.*

from Pachacamac is attached to the guest room's closet door.

By 1901 Lummis had finished a bedroom, bathroom, and vestibule at the eastern end of the house. He designed the bedroom for Eve and gave it a tiny alcove that he called Eve's tower. The room used to open to the outside, but the side door ("Eve's little postern") has since been covered over. For the fireplace Lummis wrote:

Love and a Fire
  They're easy lit;
But to keep either —
  Wood to it!

After completing the fireplace, Lummis turned his attention to a plumbing project. "Build that noble bathtub," he wrote in his journal, "and it took 2 mighty good men 12 hours steady labor, interrupted only twice for 20-minute bites of meals. But it will be just the same bathtub 10,000 years from now. I wish the plumbing and the pipes and the nickel plating would last as long!"

A doorway in the vestibule opens onto the veranda; and a steep, narrow staircase leads to the second floor, where Lummis built his daughter Turbesé's bedroom, his own study, an attic, and the upper story to the tower. The bedroom door combines two disparate elements: one of the planks given him from the old Mission San Fernando, and a keyhole plate whose stippled design suggests an ancient Peruvian fetish.

"It's a beauty," Lummis proudly said of his upstairs study. This was the famous "Lion's Den" in

Two views of Lummis's upstairs study, the Lion's Den.
HSSC Collection (top); Huntington Library (bottom).

which he did his writing. The room has hand-crafted bookcases ("hard wood & hard work"), a window seat, and a corner fireplace inscribed with the lines:

Spark, Ben-Resheph — Son of the Flame —
  Like the Man of Uz we should
Look to thy Sire, the Given Fire—
  But thy Mother is this our Wood.

The fireplace mantel, like the one in the guest room, has a frieze of clay heads from Teotihuacán.

"On one side of the study," wrote a visitor in 1905, "a narrow hole opens into an unfinished attic. Through this hole and the attic Mr. Lummis crawls to his bedchamber in the tower." Barbed wire reinforced the tower walls, a two-thousand-pound girder strengthened the floor, and twenty boulders, each weighing two hundred and fifty pounds, served as battlements. When the Southwest Museum was built, Lummis had a splendid view of its tower from one of his own tower windows.

It was not until 1904 that Lummis finished work on the west wing of El Alisal: dining room, pantry, and kitchen. The spacious dining room, or *comedor* (almost as large as the *museo*), has a corner fireplace, wall niches like those in a pueblo dwelling, and an open-beamed ceiling with corbels and herringbone planking. In the floor by the fireplace are six diamond-shaped tiles arranged to form a star. The tiles came from the ruined old Mission San Juan Capistrano, whose roof and adobe walls were repaired by Lummis's Landmarks Club. Next to the fireplace is a woodbox made by Lummis and decorated by artist

Photograph by Lummis of the sideboard he made.
It has antique doors and a window looking
out to the veranda. *HSSC Collection.*

Maynard Dixon, who pyrographed the Indian motifs of a bird, a deer, and a bear. The woodbox originally was located in the second-floor study, as was the camera cupboard door now on display downstairs. On the cupboard door is a design also pyrographed by Dixon and inspired by Lummis's photograph of the elaborately carved stone gateway at Tiahuanaco.

Lummis made several interesting pieces of furniture for the *comedor*. One cupboard has heavy shelves hewn to fit securely into wedge-shaped notches. A sideboard incorporates "a precious pair of cupboard doors" carved from Spanish cedar in the early eighteenth century. Lummis brought the old doors from Isleta in 1900 and built them into the upper part of his sideboard, where they flank a window. "Instead of the mirror other folks always put in a sideboard (God knows why)," he wrote, "this has a window, looking down the 50-foot cloister — and it is good!" As with much of his other carpentry, both sideboard and cupboard show the mark of the adze. No friend of the planing mill, as one reporter observed, Lummis preferred an irregular surface and the wavy effect that he called a moonlight finish.

The exterior of the *comedor* is as interesting as the interior. The south wall, with its curvilinear gable, houses a bell said to have come from a mission *asistencia*. The western wall features a tower-like structure, squat and sturdy, built around the dining room alcove. An Indian grinding-stone can be seen among the heavy boulders of the outer wall.

Some lively dinner parties took place in the *come-*

A Lummis photograph of the dining room.
The lamps are made from Indian baskets and
fringed with buckskin. *HSSC Collection.*

dor. For a number of years Lummis played host to members of the Order of the Mad March Hares: friends with birthdays in March. Often he entertained at what he called "Noises" and defined as an "informal Old California Good Time." Journalist Harry Carr offered another definition: "shindig of the intellectuals."

On the swinging door between dining room and pantry is a huge slice of redwood burl, a birthday gift from artist Fernand Lungren. The pantry is conveniently arranged, with many shelves, two pass-throughs for dishes, and an air cooler for food. Against one wall is a ladder to the attic, in which Lummis stored his periodicals. The kitchen, patterned after one at Mission San Juan Capistrano, took seven months to build. The walls (reinforced with barbed wire) slope upward to a vent in the high ceiling. A steep flight of stairs goes from the kitchen to the basement wine cellar, which was well stocked with claret and sauterne. One of the kitchen doors leads to the pantry, one to the patio, and a third to what Lummis described as "a nice screen breakfast room on the porch — all screen and morning glories." The porch area since has been enclosed.

In a climate where it was possible to enjoy the outdoors for at least 325 days a year, said Lummis, any well-planned house should have a patio and veranda, and he wrote articles in praise of both. The veranda at El Alisal (offering "spacious, gracious, airy coolness") extends for fifty feet along the north side of the house and is presided over by a mural of a young Isleta girl by a heap of drying corn. The mural — possibly done by Charles Russell — is sim-

63

Lummis at work with his wood chisel. *HSSC Collection.*

ilar to a picture taken by Lummis in 1888 and later incorporated in the photographic window of the *museo*.

The magisterial sycamore named *El Alcalde Mayor,* or the Chief Justice, once dominated the patio at El Alisal. Numerous social events — including Lummis's third wedding — took place beneath the sycamore's great canopy. In the name of *El Alcalde Mayor* Lummis issued subpoenas and conducted mock trials of "Hardened & Notorious Sinners" accused of "the High Misdemeanor of Not Knowing An Old California Good Time." Those receiving a summons were told: "The prosecutor is Fierce, but the Jury of 18 has been Carefully Packed in Your Favor. If you can put up any sort of defense the verdict will be 'Not Guilty, Come Again.' "

With the construction of dining room and kitchen, the house was essentially complete by 1904. Asked, however, when he expected the work to end, Lummis replied, *"Never,* I hope." As he explained to Frederick Webb Hodge, the demands of deskwork made physical labor a necessary and welcome counterpoint. "By it," he said, "I keep in good trim. Without it I sh[oul]d be dead in six months." He still had plans to build another room and a seventy-foot cloister. He also wanted to make his own tiles with which to roof El Alisal. Although he carried out none of these projects, he did build two small guest houses across the patio from the main house. One was for his daughter Bertha, born out of wedlock during his college days. He first learned of her existence in 1904 and promptly welcomed her into the family. The other little house was for his son

El Alisal patio and the little houses built for two of
the Lummis children. The tower was removed after
severe damage in the 1971 Sylmar earthquake.
HSSC Collection.

Jordan, who constructed the tower himself. (Damaged in the 1971 Sylmar earthquake, the tower had to be removed.)

One visitor to El Alisal called it "a casual higgledy-piggledy place, more uncomfortable than a tent in the wilderness." Another complained, "The museum-of-a-house was hot as a kitchen, for few of the picturesque windows will open and the doorways are narrow." The Los Angeles Chapter of the American Institute of Architects was more appreciative, making Lummis an honorary member for his work on El Alisal and his contributions to the design of the Southwest Museum.

"I have made a beautiful home worthy for my children to live in, and fit to be lived in for a thousand years," Lummis wrote in 1910 in a preamble to his will. To protect members of his family "against their own improvidence or misfortune in the future," he conveyed El Alisal to the Southwest Museum to hold in trust for his children and their descendants, "as a home and residence; subject only to the right of the public to free view of the exhibit rooms three hours a week."

The first threat to Lummis's plans came in 1912 when a number of Arroyo home owners faced condemnation of their property to make way for a park. Firing off a letter to the Park Commission, Lummis said of El Alisal: "I believe it is admitted by expert authority to be not only unique in America, but an architectural landmark any city would be glad to preserve." After describing the house and its valuable collections, Lummis concluded: "A park without a museum, a museum without a park, are both a

67

The west facade of El Alisal. *Photo by Charles Puck.*
HSSC Collection.

little less than they should be. Nothing but dynamite would obliterate this landmark. I do not believe you will feel it should be obliterated. I believe you will meet me halfway; and that in parking and beautifying the Arroyo Seco you will not destroy its first attempt — nearly a generation ago — to do this very thing." His eloquence swayed the Park Commission, and El Alisal was saved.

Lummis assumed that deeding El Alisal to the Southwest Museum would allow his children, and those who came after them, to live tax-free and rent-free, with land enough to support them. In 1923, however, the museum decided it was neither legal nor practical to commit itself to maintaining a home for the family in perpetuity. Lummis was shattered by the decision, which he felt robbed his children of their birthright. The museum did keep El Alisal for a number of years after Lummis's death in 1928, and two generations of the family continued to live there: Jordan Lummis, his wife Beatrice, and their three daughters. Divorced in 1938, Jordan moved away, but Beatrice remained at El Alisal, acting as caretaker and resident hostess until her death in 1961.

In 1939 the state acquired a narrow strip on the eastern edge of the property for a street extension. At about the same time the Southwest Museum announced that it could no longer afford the upkeep of El Alisal and must sell both house and land. "Chas. Lummis Famed Rock House Doomed," one newspaper headline read. "Friends Incensed That Loved Shrine May Be Sacrificed." The Los Angeles League of Women Voters promptly called a meet-

El Alisal in 1986, after work began on renovation of the garden. *Photo by Harry Chamberlain. HSSC Collection.*

ing to discuss ways to save the property as a historic landmark. Soon afterward the Charles Fletcher Lummis Memorial Association organized, with impresario Lynden E. Behymer as president. As a result of efforts by interested groups like these, in 1941 the legislature voted funds to acquire El Alisal. Title passed in 1943 from the museum to the state, which named the property California State Monument No. 531. The city of Los Angeles leased El Alisal from 1944 until 1971, when it became the legal owner.

City funds for opening El Alisal to the public were not budgeted until 1954. The appropriation was made after a determined campaign by former city librarian Althea Warren, who had been elected president of the Lummis Memorial Association. In 1961, following the death of longtime curator Beatrice Lummis Simmons, the Lummis Memorial Association and the Southwest Museum invited the California Historical Society to set up local headquarters in El Alisal. Four years later, when CHS moved from the Lummis Home to El Molino Viejo in San Marino, the Historical Society of Southern California made El Alisal its headquarters. During the past ten years HSSC has completed a major project at the Lummis Home: the design and planting of a waterwise demonstration garden that attracts thousands of visitors to El Alisal.

The Lummis Home Garden

A year after buying his Arroyo acreage, Lummis began to put in trees along its boundary. On three sides he planted eucalypti, and for five hundred feet on Avenue 42 he planted a lemon tree hedge. Soon the living fence enclosed a variety of other fruit trees: peaches, pears, plums, olives, loquats, and guavas. There were ornamental trees as well, including a cedar of Lebanon, a birch, and several palm-like draecenas. In 1901 Lummis planted a splendid fig tree and a sequoia in memory of his little son Amado.

"A chief charm of Southern California," Lummis wrote in 1895, "is that a new home can be framed in its own little Eden in time so short the thing seems magic." In addition to the hundreds of trees at his

73

El Alisal photographed by Lummis in 1905. The picture ("Twelve million flowers to the acre") illustrated his article "The Carpet of God's Country." *Courtesy of Southwest Museum, Los Angeles. N22042.*

arroyo Eden, Lummis had grapes, berries, melons, and vegetables. He also had an abundance of flowers, including water lilies, roses, lilacs, and iris. Wildflowers covered much of the property. "On my own little place there are, today, at least forty million wild blossoms by calculation," Lummis boasted in 1905. In a journal entry for 1913 he referred specifically to brodiaeas, which he called his favorite wildflower.

After Lummis's death, plants native to California and the Southwest were used extensively each time the garden was redesigned. The work of one man made such landscaping possible. He was Theodore Payne, an Englishman who opened a nursery in Los Angeles in 1903 and over the next fifty-seven years brought into cultivation nearly five hundred species of native flora. When the Los Angeles Department of Parks took over management of El Alisal in 1943, it had Theodore Payne choose plants for the garden and supervise their placement. Unfortunately, not every worker assigned to El Alisal understood the care of native plants, or how to distinguish them from weeds. As one former gardener recalled, seedlings often were "watered out or hoed out," and larger plants sometimes fared no better. On one occasion a foreman, with misplaced zeal, dug up manzanita, ceanothus, and a bed of desert willow.

Over the years the garden suffered from vandalism and neglect. Then in 1979, as Los Angeles prepared to celebrate the two hundredth anniversary of its founding, a bicentennial committee endorsed restoration of the garden as a special project. The Theodore Payne Foundation, which carries on the

Volunteer workers in the Lummis Home garden.
Photo by Tom Engler. HSSC Collection.

work of Mr. Payne, made a gift of native plants, city workers put them in, and volunteers from the Payne Foundation and the Historical Society of Southern California helped with weeding, trimming, and pruning. A native plant festival held at El Alisal in 1982 celebrated the new garden.

Jacquelyn Wilson, who became executive director of the Historical Society in 1980, believed the full potential of the garden had not yet been realized. She envisioned a master plan that would unify house and garden and serve as a model of historic site management. At her invitation, several landscape architecture students at Cal Poly Pomona submitted ideas for revitalizing the garden. Student suggestions for a garden requiring a minimum of irrigation captured the interest of the Historical Society board.

In 1985 the board approved redesign of the garden to demonstrate the use of water-conserving plants for residential landscaping. The Santa Monica Mountains Conservancy made a grant of $80,000 to help launch the project, which had the enthusiastic endorsement of public officials, naturalists, and botanists. Other major grants came from the Metropolitan Water District of Southern California, the Los Angeles Department of Water and Power, The Ralph M. Parsons Foundation, and the Stanley Smith Horticultural Trust of Scotland.

To design a waterwise garden, the society commissioned Robert C. Perry, professor of landscape architecture at Cal Poly Pomona and author of *Trees and Shrubs for Dry California Landscapes*. "I tried to complement the nature of the site, but also be sen-

Robert C. Perry, project architect for the Lummis Home
Water-Conserving Garden. *Photo by Margaret Dickerson.*
HSSC Collection.

sitive to the fabric of this region in terms of its climate, soils, and plant communities," Perry said of his work at El Alisal. His design has been acclaimed as adventuresome and stunning. It also is eminently practical. The garden requires only half the amount of water used for the average residential landscaping, and the meadow of rosy-red yarrow (a substitute for turf) needs mowing just three to four times a year.

Perry's design incorporates distinct areas, in which plants with similar water needs are grouped together. The entry garden frames the house with rockroses, lavender, and rosemary. A shade garden offers a cool seating space under bay trees and sycamores. A regional plant garden — requiring a minimum of maintenance and water — features olive trees, myrtles, and acacias. Still another area displays California native plants, including toyon, manzanita, ceanothus, and Fremontia. *A Companion and Guide to the Waterwise Garden*, a booklet written by Perry and published by the Historical Society, contains an annotated list of all the plants, with practical advice on their cultivation.

Curvilinear pathways through the garden have replaced the Park Department's old asphalt roadway, which in turn replaced Lummis's "wandering and unconventional foot-paths." The new paths, of decomposed granite, permit run-off water to be absorbed by the sandy soil. They also encourage visitors to stroll through the grounds. Amid the profusion of drought-resistant plants they will find a solitary rosebush. It was planted by the tower in 1987 in memory of Lummis's daughter Turbesé. The rose-

79

Garden volunteer Lois Kern with visitors to the 1988 Garden Open House. The children painted a mural using twigs and ferns as paintbrushes. *Photo by Henk Friezer. HSSC Collection.*

bush grew from a cutting of a perpetual white moss rose planted in 1880 in Amador County's Fiddletown, famous for music-making as well as mining in Gold Rush times.

When the Lummis Home Water-Conserving Garden was dedicated in April 1987, eight hundred people came for the ceremony. More than a thousand attended the garden fair at El Alisal the following year, and twice that number came in 1989. The ten thousandth visitor was welcomed in April 1994. "Anyone who says that Southern Californians are not committed to conserving water should stop by the Lummis Garden in April," remarked Thomas F. Andrews, executive director of the Historical Society. "Our guests are eager to know every detail of waterwise gardening. Our irrigation, landscaping, and gardening experts are exhausted but exhilarated by the end of the day."

Home gardeners, professional gardeners, landscape architects, and conservationists have paid tribute to the Lummis Home Water-Conserving Garden. Both Los Angeles Beautiful and the Los Angeles Conservancy have honored the garden with special awards. The Historical Society also has received a certificate of appreciation from the UCLA Extension Division for special services to faculty and students in the landscape architecture program.

As custodian of El Alisal, the Historical Society has devoted attention not only to the garden but to the house itself. Interior walls have been painted and the boulder walls repaired. Programs sponsored by the Society have restored some of the vitality that Lummis brought to El Alisal with his "Noises,"

81

Natividad Vacio and José Garcia, who often provide music for special events at El Alisal. *Photo by Margaret Dickerson. HSSC Collection.*

Spanish dinners, March Hare parties, and other celebrations. Special events, such as book signings and talks by authors, still take place in the *museo*, with refreshments served in the *comedor*. Both rooms are the setting, also, for the annual holiday open house for members. On that festive occasion musicians with guitar and mandolin play some of the old California songs collected by Lummis.

The *zaguán*, which served for a time as Lummis's office, now is the El Alisal Book Shop, which offers a large selection of books and pamphlets on California and the West. The two former bedrooms downstairs have been converted to offices for the Society. The kitchen still is put to use. (One engaging kitchen crew was a sixth-grade class studying life in early Los Angeles. With the *Landmarks Club Cook Book* as guide, the students prepared a meal that Lummis would have enjoyed.) Until a gas range was installed in the kitchen in 1904, Lummis cooked on his "camp-irons" in the patio. Under the old sycamore he entertained friends, and here the Sequoya League was founded. Lummis considered the patio an extension of the house, a pleasant area for gatherings, and it continues as such today.

Nearly one century after Lummis began work on El Alisal, it still vividly reflects the personality of its builder and his interest in the old missions of California, the pueblos of the American Southwest, and the archaeology of Mexico, Peru, and Bolivia. In the words of the Historical Society's executive director, Thomas F. Andrews: "El Alisal is a place where history lingers — just as Charles Lummis intended."

Arroyo Neighbors

El Alisal was not the only picturesque house built near the Arroyo; and Lummis — although the most flamboyant resident — was not the only lively personality or the only contributor to the world of arts and letters. Indeed so many authors and artists settled along the Arroyo Seco in the 1890s and early 1900s that critics have coined the term "Arroyo Culture."

Most people were drawn to the Arroyo by its natural beauty; a few came because of Lummis. Mary Austin, for example, spent several months in 1899 on East Avenue 41 and often visited the nearby Lummis home on East Avenue 43. Seeking literary encouragement and intellectual stimulus, she found both at El Alisal. Despite unflattering statements about Lummis in her autobiography, Mary Austin once described him as her first and warmest friend in the West. Between 1899 and 1903 Lummis pub-

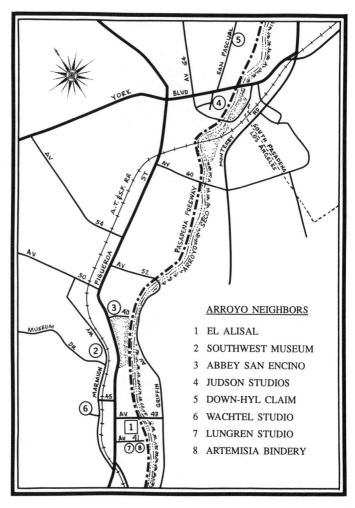

ARROYO NEIGHBORS

1 EL ALISAL
2 SOUTHWEST MUSEUM
3 ABBEY SAN ENCINO
4 JUDSON STUDIOS
5 DOWN-HYL CLAIM
6 WACHTEL STUDIO
7 LUNGREN STUDIO
8 ARTEMISIA BINDERY

Map by Miriam Campbell.

lished poems, short stories, and a novelette by Mary Austin; and in 1906 he published her eyewitness account of the San Francisco earthquake and fire.

Idah Meacham Strobridge, who moved to California in 1901, had her first stories published in *Land of Sunshine* in 1898, when she was still living in Nevada. There she managed a cattle ranch and a gold mine and worked in her Artemisia Bindery. One admiring journalist described her as "a cultured woman of the new age." In Garvanza she built a large bungalow on East Avenue 41, just a few blocks from El Alisal. She named her house "At the Sign of the Sagebrush," and in it she continued her Artemisia Bindery. Later she added a gallery, "The Little Corner of Local Art," and also displayed autographed books by local writers. The Artemisia Bindery published several books, including three by Mrs. Strobridge. Two of them were illustrated by Maynard Dixon, an occasional visitor to the Arroyo.

Artist Fernand Lungren, who moved to East Avenue 41 in 1903, shared with Lummis an interest in the Southwest and the American Indian, and shared with Mary Austin and Idah Meacham Strobridge a love of the desert. Lungren was well known for his paintings of the Southwest, commissioned by the Santa Fe Railroad to encourage tourism. In 1892, on his first visit to New Mexico, he stayed for several months with Lummis's friend Amado Chaves. The following year Lungren lived on the Hopi First Mesa, was adopted by the Clan of the Badger, and became an honorary member of the Snake-Antelope priesthood. In his large studio-bungalow in Garvanza, Lungren displayed his

Olive Percival hanging a Japanese lantern in the garden
of her half-timbered house, the Down-hyl Claim.
Courtesy of Huntington Library.

paintings and Indian relics. Lummis suggested — to no avail — that he donate his splendid collection of Navajo blankets to the Southwest Museum. The redwood burl that Lungren gave to Lummis on his forty-fifth birthday still graces the pantry door at El Alisal.

On the slopes of Mount Washington, above El Alisal, landscape artists Elmer and Marion Wachtel built a Craftsman bungalow-studio in 1906. Located on West Avenue 43, and reached by a grassy trail, it offered superb views of hills, mountains, and Arroyo. *Land of Sunshine* for March 1896 carried an appreciative article on Elmer Wachtel, whose pen and ink drawings often appeared in the magazine. His vignettes identified two departments in the magazine: one devoted to the Landmarks Club, and the other to book reviews by Lummis ("That Which Is Written"). Both Wachtels were associated with the "Eucalyptus School" of regional landscape painting, and it was said of Marion Wachtel that she could paint from memory any native tree or shrub that she had ever seen. The Wachtel Home, together with the surrounding eucalyptus grove, is a Los Angeles Historic-Cultural Monument.

In May 1899 — the same month in which Mary Austin visited the Arroyo and Lummis was framing arrowheads to display in his *museo* — Olive Percival bought a lot on San Pascual Avenue, overlooking the Arroyo. She was disdainful of El Alisal, dismissing it as unique, but not beautiful. Her idea of beauty was the two-story, half-timbered house ("the Down-hyl Claim") that she built for her mother

The Abbey San Encino, designed and built by
Clyde Browne. *Courtesy of Ward Ritchie.*

90

and herself and filled with remarkable collections of books, dolls, daguerreotypes, pewter, silver, Lalique, and Oriental art. She planted a series of charming gardens on her acre and held famous garden teas and moon-viewing parties, as well as her regular Tuesday evening at-homes. Numerous authors, artists, bibliophiles, and flower lovers visited the Down-hyl Claim and signed the "gueste bookes of Mistresse Olive Percival, Spinster." An artist at heart (an insurance clerk by profession), Miss Percival made clever designs with scissors and paper; took interesting photographs (some appeared in *Land of Sunshine*); and wrote poetry, short stories, and travel literature.

Not far from the Down-hyl Claim, on Arroyo Glen Street, printer Clyde Browne built his Abbey San Encino, which is as distinctive, romantic, and eclectic as El Alisal. Combining elements of California mission and medieval castle, it has cloisters, a belltower, chapel, minstrel gallery, and dungeon. Browne, like Lummis, used stones from the Arroyo as his principal building material; but he also used brick, tile, stained glass, and railroad ties, and he incorporated fragments gathered from historic sites in this country and abroad. Browne worked on the Abbey from 1915 to 1929; and alongside it he built a series of little stone studios that he rented to authors, artists, and craftsmen. The west wing of the Abbey housed his printshop. Among the many works he printed were some he himself had written: poems, a play, a book on the missions, and several booklets on the building of the Abbey. One of Browne's longtime clients was Occidental College,

USC's College of Fine Arts and Architecture before
it burned in 1910, and the new building (now the
Judson Studios) photographed around 1914.
Courtesy of Judson Studios.

which had moved to a site by the Arroyo in 1898. Browne delighted in the medieval and enjoyed colophons such as "Printed by Clyde Browne in the Escritorium of the Olden Abbey of San Encino in the village of Garvanza, hardby Pasadena, California." Abbey San Encino, which is still owned and occupied by the Browne family, is a Los Angeles Historic-Cultural Monument.

One of the first artists to settle by the Arroyo — and one of the most influential — was William Lees Judson, who came west in 1893 and on Thorne Street built a house whose architecture mingles Craftsman with Queen Anne. Associated with the art department of the University of Southern California for twenty-five years, Judson organized its College of Fine Arts and became its first dean. He established the college on Avenue 66, opposite his own house, and many craftsmen built their studio-homes nearby. The college site, as described in a school bulletin, was "on a cliff overlooking an unspoiled natural park, the famed Arroyo Seco, with a perennial stream and groves of magnificent trees, rocks, cliffs, and acres of boulders, wide stretches of oak-dotted sward, and the snow-capped mountains closing every vista." It is little wonder that with such a view Judson turned from portraiture to landscape painting.

The second College of Fine Arts building (the first burned down in 1910) was used not only for classes but also as a center for the Arroyo Guild. Over the entrance to the building is the guild's crest: a rising sun, a hammer in an artisan's hand, and the motto, "We Can." William Lees Judson

Drawing by Ernest Batchelder of his Pasadena house on the east bank of the Arroyo. *Courtesy of Robert W. Winter.*

was the first president of the guild, "an association
of expert workers who design and make beautiful
things." Judson wrote the lead article in the one and
only issue of the *Arroyo Craftsman* (October 1909),
which was edited by his friend George Wharton
James. James contributed an article on Indian baskets and an appreciation of Arroyo artist Hanson
Puthuff. The magazine's credo, said James, was
"simple living, high thinking, pure democracy, gen-
uine art, honest craftsmanship, natural inspiration,
and exalted aspiration." The old College of Fine
Arts building — a Los Angeles Historic-Cultural
Monument — has long been home to the Judson
Studios, founded by Judson's sons in 1897 and
known as the Tiffany's of the West.

Some artists and writers associated with the
Arroyo Culture lived beyond the borders of
Garvanza. In South Pasadena, for example, there
was Lummis's admired friend Margaret Collier
Graham: essayist, short story writer, a contributor
to *Land of Sunshine*, and vice-president of the
Landmarks Club. In Pasadena there was Lummis's
colorful rival, George Wharton James: author, editor, and lecturer, and an authority on Indian baskets
and blankets. ("Twin titans of regional culture" is
Lawrence Clark Powell's description of James and
Lummis.) Also living in Pasadena, in Craftsman
bungalows on the rim of the Arroyo, were Ernest
Batchelder, renowned for his decorative tiles; and
Jean Mannheim, whose lyrical paintings are said to
have acquainted people in every state of the Union
with the beauties of Pasadena and the Arroyo.

Who were the Arroyoans? They were poets and

95

The great sycamore around which Lummis built his home. At top center is Mary Austin, who dedicated her first book, *The Land of Little Rain*, to Eve Lummis. *Courtesy of Huntington Library.*

painters; designers and builders; teachers and editors; artisans in metal, leather, ceramics, and glass. They found stimulating companionship in Lummis's *museo* or beneath his sycamore; in the Arroyo Craftsmen Guildhall; in local galleries, studios, and gardens. For a quarter of a century the Arroyo Seco inspired a remarkable small renaissance. The Arroyo community has not forgotten its heritage. Walking tours, a local history fair, and Museums of the Arroyo Day all focus attention on the Arroyo, both past and present. High on a hill overlooking the Arroyo is the great Southwest Museum, founded by Lummis in 1907. The motto he chose for the museum applies also to El Alisal, which maintains a vital presence in the Los Angeles area: *Mañana Flor de Sus Ayeres* — Tomorrow is the flower of its yesterdays.

"The Southwesterner." Lummis in 1889, when his left arm was still paralyzed. *Courtesy of Southwest Museum, Los Angeles. N22203.*

98

Chronology

1859

Charles Fletcher Lummis is born on March 1 in Lynn, Massachusetts, to Harriet Fowler Lummis and the Reverend Henry Lummis.

1877

Lummis enters Harvard.

1878

Lummis has a summer job as a printer at the Profile House, a resort hotel in New Hampshire.

He writes, prints, and sells *Birch Bark Poems*, a miniature booklet later issued in several variant editions.

1879

Although ignorant of the fact for a quarter of a century, Lummis becomes the father of a daughter, Bertha, born to Emma Nourse, whom he had met the previous summer. The child is adopted by the Orison W. Page family of Goshen, New Hampshire.

1880

Lummis marries medical student Dorothea Rhodes.

1881

Dropping out of Harvard, Lummis moves to Chillicothe, Ohio, to manage his father-in-law's farm.

1882

Lummis becomes editor of the *Scioto Gazette* in Chillicothe.

1884

He starts on his cross-country walk from Cincinnati to Los Angeles, reporting on his progress to the *Chillicothe Leader* and the *Los Angeles Daily Times*.

1885

Lummis arrives in Los Angeles on February 1. The next day he begins work as city editor of the *Los Angeles Daily Times*.

1886

As special correspondent for the *Times*, Lummis covers the campaign of General George H. Crook against the Chiricahua Apaches in the Arizona Territory.

1887

Lummis suffers a paralytic stroke.

1888

On February 5 Lummis leaves for New Mexico, hoping to regain his health. He begins the diary that he keeps for the next forty years.

After a brief stay with the Chaves family in San Mateo, Lummis moves to the pueblo of Isleta.

In August he meets archaeologist Adolph Bandelier, with whom he explores the Southwest.

1889

Lummis survives an attempt on his life made when he antagonized a local political boss. A neighbor, Isleta schoolteacher Eve Douglas, helps nurse him back to health.

1891

Divorced from Dorothea Rhodes in February, Lummis marries Eve Douglas one month later.

1892

Turbesé Lummis is born on June 9. She receives her Indian name (meaning Sunburst, or Rainbow of the Sun) from her Isleta godmother, Marcelina Abeita.

Lummis secures the return to Isleta of schoolchildren taken from the Pueblo to be educated at the government's Indian school in Albuquerque.

Lummis settles his family in Los Angeles, and joins Bandelier on an expedition to Peru and Bolivia.

1893

Lack of funding halts the expedition, and Lummis returns to Los Angeles in December.

El Alisal photographed by Lummis in 1899. His daughter
Turbesé is standing on the upper platform at the right.
Courtesy of Huntington Library.

1894

Lummis's first son is born on November 15 and named Amado Bandelier in honor of Amado Chaves and Adolph Bandelier.

1895

The first issue of *Land of Sunshine* to be edited by Lummis appears in January.

In September Lummis buys three acres of land along the Arroyo Seco.

1897

Lummis founds the Landmarks Club for the preservation of the old California missions.

1898

Lummis begins to build El Alisal.

1900

Jordan Lummis is born on January 19 and named for Stanford president David Starr Jordan. The boy is also called Quimu (Young Mountain Lion), the name given him by Pablo Abeita of Isleta.

Amado Bandelier Lummis dies on Christmas Day.

1901

Lummis announces a new organization that will work for Indian rights.

Before President Theodore Roosevelt delivers his first message to Congress, he consults with Lummis on matters pertaining to the West.

Lummis and other members of the Warner's Ranch
Commission on the Monserrate Ranch, where the government wished to settle displaced Cupeño Indians. Lummis
helped locate a better site, with more water and more fertile
soil. *Courtesy of Southwest Museum, Los Angeles. N34302.*

1902

Lummis formally organizes the Sequoya League and becomes chairman of the Warner's Ranch Indian Advisory Commission.

Land of Sunshine is renamed *Out West* ("The Nation Back of Us, The World in Front").

Gas and electricity are installed at El Alisal.

1903

Lummis organizes the Southwest Society of the Archaeological Institute of America. One of its goals is to build a museum in Los Angeles.

Santa Clara College awards an honorary degree to Lummis for distinguished service to the history of the West.

1904

Keith Lummis, named for artist William Keith, is born on August 20.

1905

Lummis becomes Los Angeles City Librarian in June.

1906

Lummis's newfound daughter, Bertha Belle Page, comes to live at El Alisal and takes her father's name.

1907

The Southwest Museum incorporates. Lummis is named as secretary.

Breaking ground for the Southwest Museum, November 16, 1911. The three participants are Elizabeth Benton Frémont, General Adna Chaffee, and Lummis, who was blind at the time. *Courtesy of Southwest Museum, Los Angeles. N24322.*

1908

Lummis is a founding board member of the School of American Archaeology (later named the School of American Research) at Santa Fe.

1909

Eve and Lummis separate.

The November issue of *Out West* is the last to be edited by Lummis.

1910

Lummis conveys his home and special collections to the Southwest Museum.

He resigns as City Librarian.

1911

In March Lummis heads an expedition that works among the Mayan ruins in Guatemala. Jungle fever leaves him temporarily blind.

In November he takes part in the groundbreaking ceremony for the Southwest Museum.

1912

Lummis revives his column, "In the Lion's Den," for *West Coast Magazine*.

1914

The Southwest Museum opens in August.

Lummis is a founding member and vice-president of the Arroyo Seco Association, whose goal is "to

Protect, Improve and Beautify the Valley of the Arroyo Seco."

1915

In March Lummis resigns as secretary of the Southwest Museum.

He marries his secretary, Gertrude Redit, in May.

1917

Alfonso XIII of Spain makes Lummis a Knight Commander in recognition of his sympathetic writings on the role of Spain in the New World.

1923

The Southwest Museum celebrates Founder's Day in honor of Lummis and names the caracol tower for him.

1928

Lummis makes his final visit to New Mexico. On November 25 he dies at El Alisal.

1939

The Charles Fletcher Lummis Memorial Association organizes to work for the preservation of El Alisal.

1943

Title to El Alisal passes from the Southwest Museum to the state of California, which names the property a state monument.

Liberty Ship 182 is named for Charles Fletcher Lummis.

1944

The state leases El Alisal to the Los Angeles Department of Parks for a period of twenty-five years.

1955

The Lummis Memorial Association plants four saplings to replace the great four-trunked sycamore, which died of old age.

1961

The California Historical Society opens its Southern California office in El Alisal.

1965

El Alisal becomes the headquarters of the Historical Society of Southern California.

1968

The New Mexico Folklore Society adds the name of Charles Fletcher Lummis to its roll of honor.

1970

The Cultural Heritage Board of the city of Los Angeles declares the Lummis Home a historic monument.

1971

The state transfers ownership of El Alisal to the city of Los Angeles, for use as a public park and historic monument.

1979

Volunteer workers in the Historical Society begin renovation of the garden. The Theodore Payne Foundation makes a donation of native plants in honor of the upcoming Los Angeles bicentennial.

1985

The board of the Historical Society approves redesigning the garden to demonstrate the use of water-conserving plants for residential landscaping. The Santa Monica Mountains Conservancy awards a grant toward the redesign and restoration of the garden. Professor Robert C. Perry is named project architect.

1986

Ground is broken for the Lummis Home Garden Project.

1987

Eight hundred people attend the formal dedication of the garden.

A white rose is planted in honor of Turbesé Lummis Fiske, who grew up in the house and visited it often in later years.

1989

Los Angeles Beautiful gives a special award to the Historical Society for developing a water-conservation garden at El Alisal.

1992

The Los Angeles Conservancy recognizes the Lummis Home Water-Conserving Garden with a preservation award.

1994

The eighth annual garden fair at El Alisal welcomes its ten thousandth visitor.

Summons:

QUIEN A BUEN ARBOL SE ARRIMA, BUENA SOMBRA LE COBIJA

EL ALCALDE MAYOR

The Alcalde Mayor, or Chief Justice, was the historic head of the Pueblo of Our Lady, Queen of Angels. And still is, if you do but know.

Today, the Alcalde Mayor is a vast sycamore that was here when the Pueblo began in 1781. Under its four-fold spread, 100 feet each way, there gather upon occasion (and YOU are an Occasion) some of those that knew and still love the Old Days, and try to Hold them. It is the only Family ever Elected---its children Picked Ripe, so as to avoid disappointment in their growing up. They stand for many things in the progressive city and state of today; but they mean to RIDE Progress, instead of being trampled by it. Once in a while they Pause Long Enough to Live.

It is about the Last Stand of the Frontier---of the old Patriarchal Days. We cannot entertain every stranger, as was done then; but we ARE here to welcome, unto the old hospitality, those who ARE NOT STRANGERS---and You are Not. This is on purpose for YOU. Just because we like you for what you have done.

If you think an old California dinner in an old California house, with old California music and old California hearts, would be as Californian and as pleasant as the modern city---wire to Charles F. Lummis, 200 East Avenue 43, Los Angeles, Cal., (Home Phone 31553) Escribano.

The Alguacil will produce you before this honorable court, (where the Jury is packed in your favor), and will be responsible for your safe return to your bondsmen, hotel or other place of imprisonment.

If you have Appendices---bring them. They are safe from being Cut.
Come on in---the chile is fine!
In the name of the Alcalde Mayor *Chas. F. Lummis*

ESCRIBANO

NO RIOTOUS RAIMENT

HSSC Collection.

A book branded by Lummis. *HSSC Collection.*

Books by
Charles Fletcher Lummis

Birch Bark Poems. [1878.]

The Home of Ramona. Los Angeles: Charles F. Lummis & Co., 1886.

A New Mexico David and Other Stories and Sketches of the Southwest. New York: C. Scribner's Sons, 1891.

Some Strange Corners of Our Country. New York: The Century Co., 1892.

A Tramp Across the Continent. New York: C. Scribner's Sons, 1892.

The Land of Poco Tiempo. New York: C. Scribner's Sons, 1893.

The Spanish Pioneers. Chicago: A. C. McClurg & Co., 1893.

The Man Who Married the Moon, and Other Pueblo Indian Folk-Stories. New York: The Century Co., 1894.

The Gold Fish of Gran Chimú. Boston and New York: Lamson, Wolffe & Co., 1896.

The Enchanted Burro: Stories of New Mexico and South America. Chicago: Way and Williams, 1897.

The King of the Broncos, and Other Stories of New Mexico. New York: C. Scribner's Sons, 1897.

The Awakening of a Nation: Mexico Today. New York and London: Harper & Bros., 1898.

Pueblo Indian Folk-Stories. New York: The Century Co., 1910.

My Friend Will. Chicago: A. C. McClurg & Co., 1911.

In Memory of Juan Rodríguez Cabrillo, Who Gave the World California. Chula Vista: Denrich Press, 1913.

Spanish Songs of Old California. San Francisco: Scholz, Erickson & Co., 1923.

Mesa, Cañon and Pueblo: Our Wonderland of the Southwest. New York and London: The Century Co., 1925.

A Bronco Pegasus. Boston and New York: Houghton Mifflin Co., 1928.

The Spanish Pioneers and the California Missions. Chicago: A. C. McClurg & Co., 1929.

Flowers of Our Lost Romance. Boston and New York: Houghton Mifflin Co., 1929.

Collected Articles by Charles Fletcher Lummis

Bullying the Moqui. Edited by Robert Easton and Mackenzie Brown. Prescott: Prescott College Press, 1968. [Lummis articles that originally appeared in *Out West*, April to October 1903.]

Dateline Fort Bowie: Charles Fletcher Lummis Reports on an Apache War. Edited, annotated, and with an introduction by Dan L. Thrapp. Norman: University of Oklahoma Press, 1979.

General Crook and the Apache Wars. Edited by Turbesé Lummis Fiske. Flagstaff: Northland Press, 1966. [Selected dispatches to the *Los Angeles Times* April to May 1886.]

Letters from the Southwest, September 20, 1884, to March 14, 1885. Edited by James W. Byrkit. Tucson: University of Arizona Press, 1989. [Letters written to the *Chillicothe Leader.*]

Charles Fletcher Lummis:
A Selected Bibliography

Bingham, Edwin R. *Charles F. Lummis, Editor of the Southwest*. San Marino: Huntington Library, 1955.

Donnan, Christopher B. "Lummis at Tiahuanaco." *Masterkey* 47 (July–Sept. 1973): 85–93.

Fiske, Turbesé Lummis and Keith Lummis. *Charles F. Lummis: The Man and His West*. Norman: University of Oklahoma, 1975.

Gordon, Dudley. *Crusader in Corduroy*. Los Angeles: Cultural Assets Press, 1972.

Houlihan, Patrick T. and Betsy E. Houlihan. *Lummis in the Pueblos*. Flagstaff: Northland Press, 1986.

Kinsey, Ron R. "Photographic Windows at El Alisal." *Masterkey* 52 (July–Sept. 1978): 93–100.

Moneta, Daniela P., ed. *Chas. F. Lummis: The Centennial Exhibition*. Los Angeles: Southwest Museum, 1985.

Powell, Lawrence Clark. "Charles Fletcher Lummis. *The Land of Poco Tiempo*." In *Southwest Classics*. Pasadena: Ward Ritchie Press, 1974.

Powell, Lawrence Clark. "Charles Fletcher Lummis. *Land of Sunshine.*" In *California Classics: The Creative Literature of the Golden State.* Los Angeles: Ward Ritchie Press, 1971.

Sarber, Mary A. *Charles F. Lummis: A Bibliography.* Tucson: University of Arizona, 1977.

Williams, Bradley B. "Charles F. Lummis: Crusader with a Camera." *History of Photography* 5 (July 1981): 207–221.

Lummis at El Alisal around 1920.
HSSC Collection.

Lummis photograph of Rosendo Uruchurtu making a wax-cylinder recording at El Alisal. *Courtesy of Southwest Museum, Los Angeles. N24310.*

118

Index

"Mad as a M³ Chere."

"Tho this be Madness,
Yet there's
Method in it."

The Burrow.

Dear Bunny:
 The hounds are after you, and the April Fools next. Here's the only safe place!
 Postpone Death, Marriage, Taxes, and all other Disasters, particularly Your Own, and scurry to this Warren at Rabbit Time, 6 p. m. ~~Sharp~~

Sunday Mch 2 1919

 Cabbage at 6. Madness begins later. Others almost as crazy will assist. Bring your Birthday with you. If it isn't right, We will remedy it. It's not Your Fault. Wear your own Hare. Rats barred. Ears up. Check your sorrows at the door, and close the check. Don't get Mad till you have to - but then get Good and Marchy
   Chas. F. Summis-
   The Grey Hare.

Invitation to a party honoring friends with birthdays in March.
Courtesy of Southwest Museum, Los Angeles. N24539

123

250 copies
of a special edition
designed by Ward Ritchie and
printed by Premier Printing Corporation
have been signed by the author
and the designer.